for zoe serafina

Our fancy rainbow girl

do you know the sound
that i love the Best?

i hear it When i Put my
head on your chest.

there's a drum Beat in there
that fills Me With pride,
But once it Was hurting
and Quiet inside.

i'll tell you a story
about your fancy heart.
it was special to me

right from the start.

We all had such dreams of who you would be.
Your family's top Question: "a he or a she?!"

We all gathered round
to see our surprise,
and we each
fell in love
when you
opened
your
eyes.

You were here! and so precious.
Who could ask for more?
But then we heard something
we had to explore.

the doctors, they listened,
they looked, and they knew
that something was different
on the inside of you.

the sound was
so different,
so unique and
so rare,
they wanted to see
what was going on
in there.

So they whisked you away
to a clean and Bright room
to discover the Secret
of this fancy new tune.

they saw
in
your
chest
how
amazing
you are!

the sound
that they
heard
it was
never
heard
Before.

and that's when they saw it
and "oh no!" they all gasped.
"this sound is so Beautiful,
But it will not last!"

"it's tired!"
they said,
and they
knew what
to do.
they
reached
down
inside
so that
they
could
help you.

Big smiles,
we all had
when they
patched
you up tight
and we knew
that
your music
would now
stay
Just
right.

Sometimes it takes work
-the uniqueness in you-
But we're all here to help
Because we love your tune

this sound
that is yours,
you make it
alone
and inside
of you
is it's
only home.

You keep it Beating
this only-you sound

and so it is Precious
For there's Just one around.

it's a treasure you keep
right there in your chest

it must Be protected
and you do that Best.

Your tune tells
the story
that
you're
Brave
and
you're
strong
and it
fills me
with hope
when i hear your song.

Our Story–

Zoe was born on April 23rd 2011. She is the little sister to two big brothers and we were all so excited to have her. Shortly after she was born the hospital staff noticed she was having trouble breathing. Zoe was monitored in the NICU for a week while they thought she was getting stronger. She worked so hard that week, but eventually it was all too much for her. The doctors finally decided to check out her heart. They discovered a small Atrial Septal Defect a small valve, an interrupted aortic arch and a 10mm Ventricular Septal Defect. Zoe had open heart surgery at 11 days old. She showed her strength and determination throughout her recovery and finally came home to us nearly a month after she was born. She continues to be monitored, but leads an inspiring life that proves everyday that she is strong and capable and that the world needs her in it. She lives up to her name, which means LIFE!

Your Story

Each person with a Congenital Heart Anomaly has their own unique story and it deserves to be told. We have provided some space to help make this book include your story as well.

Your Story

Heart Hero's Name:

Heart Hero's Birthday:

Heart Hero's Anomalies:

About the Initial Diagnosis:

Your Story

Heart Procedures:

Hospitalizations:

Support People:

Your Story

Pictures, details, or special memories that are important to you.

www.ingramcontent.com/pod-product-compliance
Lightning Source LLC
LaVergne TN
LVHW072112070426
835509LV00003B/133